Science Fair Winners

JUNKYARD SCIENCE

20 projects and experiments about junk,
garbage, waste, things we don't need anymore,
and ways to recycle or reuse it—or lose it

by Karen Romano Young

Illustrations by David Goldin

NATIONAL GEOGRAPHIC

WASHINGTON, D.C.

credits

PUBLISHED BY THE NATIONAL GEOGRAPHIC SOCIETY
John M. Fahey, Jr., *President and Chief Executive Officer*
Gilbert M. Grosvenor, *Chairman of the Board*
Tim T. Kelly, *President, Global Media Group*
John Q. Griffin, *Executive Vice President; President, Publishing*
Nina D. Hoffman, *Executive Vice President; President, Book Publishing Group*
Melina Gerosa Bellows, *Executive Vice President, Children's Publishing*

PREPARED BY THE BOOK DIVISION
Nancy Laties Feresten, *Vice President, Editor in Chief, Children's Books*
Jonathan Halling, *Director of Design, Children's Publishing*
Jennifer Emmett, *Executive Editor, Children's Books*
Carl Mehler, *Director of Maps*
R. Gary Colbert, *Production Director*
Jennifer A. Thornton, *Managing Editor*

STAFF FOR THIS BOOK
Priyanka Lamichhane, *Editor*
James Hiscott, Jr., *Art Director*
Project Design Company, *Designer*
Grace Hill, *Associate Managing Editor*
Lewis R. Bassford, *Production Manager*
Susan Borke, *Legal and Business Affairs*

MANUFACTURING AND QUALITY MANAGEMENT
Christopher A. Liedel, *Chief Financial Officer*
Phillip L. Schlosser, *Vice President*
Chris Brown, *Technical Director*
Nicole Elliott, *Manager*
Rachel Faulise, *Manager*
Robert Barr, *Manager*

Many of the projects in this book involve human or animal subjects. The International Science and Engineering Fair (ISEF) rules include specific requirements for these types of projects. Students should familiarize themselves generally with the ISEF rules as well as the rules specific to animal and human subjects. Students also need to complete all necessary documents to ensure their project complies with the ISEF requirements. Students who have questions should seek clarification from their teachers.

You can find additional information on the ISEF website:
www.societyforscience.org/isef/about/index.asp
www.societyforscience.org/isef/rules/rules7.pdf
www.societyforscience.org/isef/rules/rules10.pd

The National Geographic Society is one of the world's largest nonprofit scientific and educational organizations. Founded in 1888 to "increase and diffuse geographic knowledge," the Society works to inspire people to care about the planet. It reaches more than 325 million people worldwide each month through its official journal, *National Geographic*, and other magazines; National Geographic Channel; television documentaries; music; radio; films; books; DVDs; maps; exhibitions; school publishing programs; interactive media; and merchandise. National Geographic has funded more than 9,000 scientific research, conservation and exploration projects and supports an education program combating geographic illiteracy. For more information, visit nationalgeographic.com.

For more information, please call 1-800-NGS LINE (647-5463) or write to the following address:
National Geographic Society
1145 17th Street N.W.
Washington, D.C. 20036-4688 U.S.A.

Visit us online at www.nationalgeographic.com/books
For librarians and teachers: www.ngchildrensbooks.org
More for kids from National Geographic: kids.nationalgeographic.com

For information about special discounts for bulk purchases, please contact National Geographic Books Special Sales: ngspecsales@ngs.org

For rights or permissions inquiries, please contact National Geographic Books Subsidiary Rights: ngbookrights@ngs.org

Library of Congress Cataloging-in-Publication Data

Young, Karen Romano.
Science fair winners : junkyard science : 20 projects and experiments about junk, garbage, waste, things we don't need anymore, and ways to recycle or reuse it -- or lose it. / by Karen Romano Young ; illustrations by David Goldin. -- 1st ed. p. cm.
   Includes index.
   ISBN 978-1-4263-0689-1 (trade pbk. : alk. paper)
   ISBN 978-1-4263-0690-7 (library binding : alk. paper)
1. Science projects--Juvenile literature. 2. Salvage (Waste, etc.)--Juvenile literature. 3. Science--Study and teaching (Elementary)--Activity programs. I. Goldin, David, ill. II. Title.
Q163.Y579 2010
628.4'45078--dc22   2009048212

Printed in the United States of America

10/WOR/1

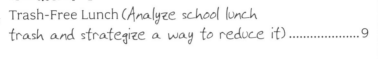

THE WORKSHOPS

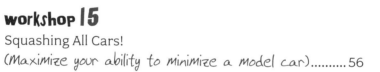

WELCOME TO JUNKYARD SCIENCE

the introduction

JUNKYARD SCIENCE is dedicated to helping you design a science fair project that will wow your teachers, the crowd at your science fair, and anyone else who hears about it.

The projects in *Junkyard Science* let you work with things that are broken, being thrown out, being recycled, rotting, or otherwise going to waste, and to get inside the heads—and toolboxes—of experts in the field.

This book will get you involved with the dumpster diving, recycling research, and trash talking that scientists do to assess how well we're taking care of our ecosystem. In the process you will sharpen your own skills and figure out what dirty diapers, lunchtime trash, and other odorific objects show about the environment and people's impact on it.

You'll learn to:

- ask a question and turn it into a project
- make observations, make comparisons, and draw conclusions (the building blocks of the scientific method), which will lead you to...

- do your own research based on the work of scientists who are doing great projects in the fields of urban archaeology (biology, social psychology, geography, entomology, and more), criminology (how crime relates to trash), physics (what happens when trash speeds through space), and geophysics (which includes the science of crushing things)—to help you get the broadest understanding of what a 21st-century trashologist needs to know.

which workshop?

Some of the workshops are experiments, because lots of science fairs require you to do an experiment. Some of them are observations and surveys, because real scientists don't just do experiments. Their work also falls into the two categories of observation and surveying. Here are ways to think about the differences:

You **experiment** when you change something in a situation and observe and survey the outcome.

You **observe** when you study a water sample, check the weather pages, and try to figure out whether a recent storm contributed to what you find in the water.

You **survey** when you look to see what trash has been left alongside a riverbank.

Some of the workshops seem really science-y. Some of them don't. This might be because you define science in terms of nature: biology (the study of life), chemistry (the elements), or physics (time, space, motion, and matter). But this book includes workshops that look at clues through the eyes of social scientists, too. Social science includes psychology (what's in someone's head), sociology (how a group and members of a group behave), anthropology (the study of humans), and economics (the science of money and business).

Some of the workshops seem hard, and some seem easy. This might depend on what you find easy to do and what challenges you. It's all good science, based on real studies and experiments. If you're not sure whether it will satisfy your teacher's requirements, ask before you get started.

What if...? I wonder...?
How can I find out...?

These three question starters are the beginnings of all science. They lead to observing, experimenting, reaching a conclusion, and finding another question, which leads you to more science and more watching, testing, and understanding, which leads to another question. . . . Well, you get the idea.

what is trashology?

It's not really a science in itself. But studying trash (trashology) leads to lots of other sciences and science concepts: chemistry and physics (what the trash is made of), water cycle (what moves the trash), geography (where the trash comes from, where it goes), economics (what creates the trash), and sociology (how people behave with their trash), and so on. So trashology is one way of getting the big picture about how we create waste and what we do with it.

what does it mean to be green?

Being green means you use products and implement practices that create the least waste, take the least

> ## " Think *globally*. Act *locally*. "
>
> — popular bumper sticker

energy, and cause the least harm to the Earth. Scientists know that human activities change the way the Earth's systems work, so being green is also a necessity if we want to save our planet. With the green movement, people are becoming more aware of the Earth's plight, and many are passionate about changing the way we live.

get the stats

People are amazed—and changed—when they realize how their day-to-day activities, or environmental footprint, impacts the Earth. Does it matter? Yes. National statistics show that our daily habits contribute greatly to our planet's environmental

troubles. Many of the projects in this book involve gathering information or samples in a small area, which will help you get a sense of how human activities are impacting that area. Science involves the study of samples, and scientists look for proof that what they've found on a small scale is also true on a larger scale. In your studies, compare small-scale and large-scale statistics through these workshops:

- Workshop 3: Sorting the Recycling
- Workshop 9: The Dirty Dozen
- Workshop 11: Baking With Sunshine

Visualize It! Lots of people are visual learners. Here are a few workshops that emphasize visuals:

- Workshop 1: Trash-Free Lunch
- Workshop 7: Waste Reduction
- Workshop 17: Up on the Roof

Be Informed! People want to know more about what's going on in the environment and how to take better care of the Earth every day. One way you can help is to let them know your findings. Another is to offer advice on how to manage trash and recycling more efficiently. These workshops include opportunities to communicate with audiences about methods you discover.

- Workshop 2: Alive, Dead, or On the Way Out?
- Workshop 12: Trash in Your Path
- Workshop 18: Diaper Dan

TRASH-FREE LUNCH

(Analyze school lunch trash and strategize a way to reduce it)

the basics

ACCORDING TO the National Solid Waste Management Association, each American creates about 4.6 pounds of trash a day. Fifty-four percent of our garbage goes to landfills, including 45 percent of all the paper we use.

TIME NEEDED ›
about a week (including the day of the trash-free lunch and the planning days preceding it)

SCIENCE ›
social science, anthropology, environmental science

SCIENCE CONCEPT ›
waste management

ADULT INVOLVEMENT ›
cooperation of your teachers, the school's administration, the cafeteria staff, and parents of all students involved

the buzz

Once a month the trash can at Sarah Noble Intermediate School in New Milford, Connecticut, is turned upside down and nobody is allowed to put anything into it. According to the students of Ms. Gill-Rogers, everyone must bring or buy food that generates no trash. At first the students found out that the lunch that generated the most trash was the one created by the school cafeteria, which objected to this monthly activity! That has changed now, as the school has found ways to reduce trash.

the lingo

assess—count or estimate
analyze—find relationships, such as cause and effect
evaluate—examine something based on specific criteria, such as material or use

the QUESTION >> Can your school's lunch trash be reduced?

the PLAN >> Assess the amount of garbage generated by lunch at your school. Then lead a trash-free lunch day and evaluate its effects on people, energy use, and the environment.

you'll need

a scale
a calculator
lunch garbage from one day's lunch at your school

OPTIONAL: *counters (the kind with a button to push each time someone puts something in the garbage, available at office supply stores)*

what to do

BEFORE DAY ONE:

1 **PLAN YOUR OBSERVATION.** What do you want to learn about the trash your school generates at lunchtime? Plan how you can find the answers to questions like the ones below. You might need to ask other students to help you observe. Use a notebook to record your answers.

- How many people get hot lunch?
- How many people bring a bag lunch?
- How many people throw out trash?
- What is getting thrown out? Food? Paper? Other?

2 **DECIDE ON STATIONS** for observations and assign observers.

For example, you might want to ask one friend to count the number of students eating lunch and their type of lunch as they enter the cafeteria, while other friends monitor garbage bins to count users and observe the type of garbage they throw out.

 DISCUSS YOUR INTENTIONS with your teacher and principal and get permission. Involve school custodians in your plans so they don't toss the trash before you've evaluated it!

OPTIONS:

* You might also consider (with permission) doing a spot assessment of the garbage to analyze how much of each type of garbage is thrown out.
* Plan, create, and get permission to give a questionnaire to students after lunch. You might ask students to list what was in their lunch, to estimate how much of it they ate, to describe the garbage it generated (food? packaging?), and to state what they did with the garbage. A questionnaire can add important data to your study.

BEFORE LUNCH, DAY ONE

4 **EAT YOUR LUNCH** early on the day you make your study of the cafeteria so that you can focus on your observation.

5 **WEIGH AN EMPTY** cafeteria garbage bin. You will subtract this weight later when you weigh the full bin to get the weight of the garbage.

6 **SET UP YOUR** observers at their stations and give them their instructions, as well as paper and pens with which to take notes. If you use counters, hand them out as well.

DURING LUNCH

7 **GATHER INFORMATION,** following your plan.

AFTER LUNCH

8 **WEIGH EACH FULL** garbage bin. Subtract the weight of the empty bin to get the weight of the trash.

9 **COLLECT YOUR DATA** from your observers. Tally the results for each station and in total.

OPTIONS:

* Hand out your questionnaire. Collect the questionnaires and tally the results.
* Go through a selected garbage bin to analyze, count, and weigh the different types of trash.

BEFORE DAY TWO

1 **CREATE A PLAN** for trash-free lunch day. Help the cafeteria staff come up with a way to serve lunch without generating trash. If your school has a trash-free lunch day, you might also choose another day, depending on the level of cooperation you are getting from the cafeteria staff. You may also make this a schoolwide program, or do it with one class.

2 **WRITE AND PRINT** menus for lunches people can bring from home that do not generate trash. Tell everyone that garbage bins will be turned upside down and that there will be no place to put trash. The goal will be to come up with lunches that can be transported to school and eaten with the least amount of paper or food waste.

3 **WORK WITH THE** cafeteria staff to create a menu that can be served on dishes brought from home or that does not require paper and other waste.

4 **PLAN HOW TO** gather data. Since you will not have trash being placed in the garbage bins, you won't need stations or helpers this time. The way to get information is through direct observation and questionnaires. Find out what people used to carry their lunches and what ingredients they brought to minimize garbage. Ask people what they're taking home in their lunch boxes, bags, or backpacks. Ask them what will have to be washed at home. Ask what food did not get eaten.

WORKSHOP RESOURCE >>

Waste-Free Lunches
http://www.wastefreelunches.org/

Would you want to make trash-free lunch a regular event at your school? Would you want it to happen every day?

CONSIDER THIS! PRESENT THIS!

Create a plan for trash-free lunch and propose it to your school, your teacher, or your principal. Use your data to support your proposal.

GO THE EXTRA MILE! Get help making posters and printing menus to inform people and help them plan for Trash-Free Lunch days.

ALIVE, DEAD, OR ON THE WAY OUT?

(Measure and compare the "juice" and cost-effectiveness of batteries)

the basics

A BATTERY IS an array or stack of voltaic cells that are arranged in such a way that they can store a certain amount of electricity, releasing it when needed.

TIME NEEDED > a week

SCIENCE > electronics, economics

SCIENCE CONCEPTS > voltage, effect of weather conditions on electronics

ADULT INVOLVEMENT > you may need some financial assistance and a ride to the store

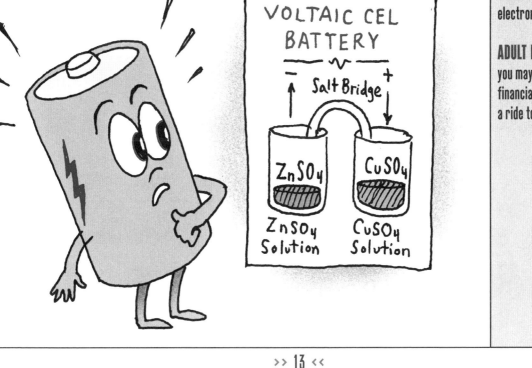

VOLTAIC CEL BATTERY

Salt Bridge

$ZnSO_4$

$CuSO_4$

$ZnSO_4$ Solution

$CuSO_4$ Solution

the buzz

Americans buy three billion batteries a year, and almost 90 percent of them wind up in landfills, where their metals may leach into groundwater.

the lingo

primary cell batteries—one-use only. **rechargeable batteries**—secondary cells. Rechargeable batteries may have different chemistries, including nickel-cadmium (NiCad) or nickel-metal hydride (NiMH). Their electrochemical cells store energy that can be used up and then restored by inserting them in a charger that is plugged into an electrical source.

the QUESTION >>

Is it environmentally and economically wise to use rechargeable batteries?

the PLAN >>

Compare the length of life of batteries under different conditions.

you'll need

a flashlight—(or several flashlights of the same kind and size, to make the experiment go faster)
batteries of different types—rechargeable and one-use—and different brands of the same size to power the flashlight. Be sure you have enough of each kind for the flashlight. That is, if four batteries are required to make the flashlight work, use four of the same type and brand. Buy all the batteries at the same time. If you have enough of one type and brand of battery lying around the house, you can add them to the experiment as a comparison. Be sure to also buy new ones of this sort for the purpose of comparing old and new.
a voltmeter—(available at electronics stores, or borrow one from your science or shop teacher)
a watch or clock
permanent marker

what to do

1 **USING THE PERMANENT** marker, label each battery with a number.

2 **USE THE VOLTMETER** to check the voltage of each battery.

3 **INSTALL THE BATTERIES** in the flashlight. Again, be sure they are all of the same type and brand and that they were bought at the same time.

4 **TAKE CAREFUL NOTE** of the time, and turn on the flashlight. If you are using several flashlights at once, take careful note of the time you turn on each one.

5 **TAKE NOTE OF** the time the flashlight goes out and switch the flashlight off.

6 **REMOVE THE BATTERIES** from the flashlight and measure their voltage using the voltmeter. Record the voltage for each battery.

WORKSHOP RESOURCES >>

> Disposal of batteries:

Environmental Protection Agency Universal Waste Rule website
http://www.epa.gov/epawaste

Search for local battery recycling by zip code at Earth 911
http://earth911.org/recycling/battery-recycling

> For more about batteries:

Battery Power
http://inventors.about.com/library/inventors/blbattery.htm

How Stuff Works: Battery
www.howstuffworks.com/battery.htm

"How Batteries Work," by Energizer
http://www.energizer.com/learning-center/Pages/how-batteries-work.aspx

When you recharge batteries, do they recharge to the same voltage level as they did when they were new?

CONSIDER THIS! PRESENT THIS!

Create a graph for each battery to show the variations in their loss of juice.

GO THE EXTRA MILE! After an hour, switch the flashlight back on again. Does it light? Try again after 12 hours, and after 24 hours. Some batteries regain a little juice after seeming to die. Measure this amount of time, too.

SORTING THE RECYCLING

(Find out what's in your kitchen)

TIME NEEDED >
a weekend

SCIENCE > economics

SCIENCE CONCEPTS >
recycling, consumer
habits, technology

ADULT INVOLVEMENT >
You may need a ride
or an escort to the
grocery store or
recycling center for
your research. The
adults in your house
may or may not be
receptive to changing
their buying habits; you
may have to get involved
in psychology and
advertising as well.

the basics

RECYCLABLE PLASTICS have different compositions and uses. Some are easier to recycle than others because of their materials. See the lingo box for more.

the buzz

Since 1976 plastic has been the most widely used material in the United States. It is the fourth biggest category of material found in landfills.

the lingo

When you look at the bottom of a plastic container, you'll find a number in a triangle. This number indicates the type of plastic that was used to make the container. Here is a list of each type of plastic and the containers created from them:

#1 polyethylene terephthalate (PET or PETE) products—Soft drink bottles, medicine containers

#2 high-density polyethylene (HDPE) products—Toys, bottles for milk, water, detergent, shampoo, motor oil

#3 polyvinyl chloride (V or PVC) products—Pipe, meat wrap, cooking oil bottles

#4 low-density polyethylene (LDPE) products—Wrapping films, grocery bags

#5 polypropylene (PP) products—Syrup bottles, yogurt tubs, diapers

#6 polystyrene (PS) products—Coffee cups, clamshell take-out containers

#7 other (usually polycarbonate) products—Medical storage containers, some Nalgene water bottles

the QUESTION >> How many of the food packages in your kitchen are made of plastic that you can recycle in your area?

the PLAN >> Assess the plastic in your kitchen and categorize it by number. Figure out how much of it can be recycled. Create a plan to minimize plastics that can't be recycled.

you'll need

your kitchen
a visit to the **grocery store**
a visit to the **recycling center** or its website, or a phone call to your town or city **department of public works**, or a phone call to the **service that collects your recycling**

what to do

1 **ASSESS THE CONTENTS** of your kitchen. Get everything in a plastic container out of the cupboards. Sort the containers according to the numbers on the bottom. Make a record of what you find.

2 **LEARN WHAT NUMBER** plastics can be recycled in your area. Call the department of public works, check the Internet, or visit the recycling center. Make a list of what can be recycled and what can't. Ask

Talk to your family about replacing nonrecyclable items. What are the arguments for and against changing?

CONSIDER THIS! PRESENT THIS!

Make a chart of items that come in nonrecyclable containers, alongside options that might replace these items in your household. Note the pros and cons of making each change: consider habit, tradition, taste, quality, price, and other factors.

GO THE EXTRA MILE! Does your state or province have a bottle bill? As of January 2010, 11 states and 8 Canadian provinces had laws that placed a refundable deposit on beverage bottles. You pay the deposit when you buy the drink; the bottle can be returned for money. States have seen average decreases in drink-bottle litter of 78 percent, and overall litter dropped 39 percent.

what people are supposed to do with plastics that can't be recycled in your area. Can you take them to another area? Or are they just supposed to go into the dump or landfill?

3 **TAKE YOUR LIST** of recyclable numbers back home to the kitchen. Establish which items come in packaging that can't be recycled. Learn about these materials, doing Internet research to find out what they're made of and whether they are recyclable in other areas.

4 **MAKE A LIST** of items that come in nonrecyclable containers. Visit the grocery store to figure out whether these items could be replaced with others found in containers that can be recycled in your area.

WORKSHOP RESOURCES >>

National Geographic Green Guide to kitchen plastics
http://www.thegreenguide.com/reports/product.mhtml?id=44

Bottle Bill Resource Guide
www.bottlebill.org

PAPER OR PLASTIC?

(Compare the decomposition rates of grocery bags)

the basics

PAPER BAGS are made of kraft paper. This type of paper is formed in paper mills as wood chips are heated in chemical solutions under pressure. The process uses more than four times the energy it takes to produce plastic bags. Plastic bags are made of a polymer called high-density polyethylene (HDPE). Each year Americans throw away about 100 billion plastic bags.

TIME NEEDED > a week, a month, or a year

SCIENCE > biology, chemistry

SCIENCE CONCEPTS > polymer construction, decomposition

ADULT INVOLVEMENT > none

the buzz

Americans use 100 billion plastic bags a year. According to the Sierra Club, four out of five grocery bags used in the United States are plastic.

the lingo

polymer—a chain made up of clumps of carbon, hydrogen, and oxygen, and sometimes silicon. Organic polymers can be made from natural cellulose that comes from plant materials.

you'll need

one **paper bag** and one **plastic bag** from a grocery store
petri dishes or small Pyrex bowls or pie plates. You'll need one for each type of material that may aid in decomposition (mulch chips, leaves, dirt, sand, water, clay, etc.)

ruler
calculator
microscope or magnifying lens
camera
notebook or computer for recording data

what to do:

1 **FIND A PLACE** where your materials can sit side by side, so you can compare them to see what happens when they are exposed to the same conditions and materials.

2 **GET A BASELINE** (beginning conditions of your materials):
a. Cut squares of your materials that are the same width and length. Calculate their area and enter the information in a notebook or database.
b. Examine your materials under a microscope or magnifying lens.
c. Photograph your materials.

3 **OVER TIME, EXPOSE** your materials to different conditions. Always expose all materials to the same conditions at the same time and for the same length of time. Conditions may include full sunlight, water, heat, cold, dirt, mulch, etc. Carefully record what you do.

4 **AFTER THE AMOUNT** of time you have designated for

the QUESTION >> Which decompose quicker: plastic or paper bags?

the PLAN >> You'll experiment with the decomposition of paper and plastic grocery bags in sun, water, and dirt. What happens to them over time? How do they change? Does anything come to them to colonize? Which material breaks down faster?

> *Strictly speaking, a* **biodegradable plastic is one which will degrade,** *or disappear back to carbon dioxide and water if left in the atmospheric zone,* **whereas other plastics won't.**

— Dr. Peter Barham

University of Bristol (England) in an interview at The Naked Scientist website.

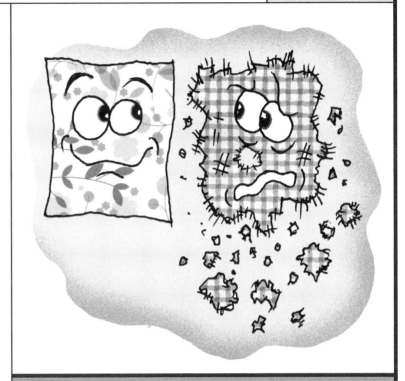

How do the decomposition rates of your materials compare with one another? What can (or can't) be done to affect the decomposition rates of different materials?

experimentation, remove all mulch, water, etc. from your experiment and examine the materials. Repeat steps 2a, 2b, and 2c with them for comparison.

WORKSHOP RESOURCES >>

• *Reusable Bags: www.resuablebags.com*
• *Grassroots Recycling Network, Grocery Bags page:* http://www.grrn.org/resources/bag_reuse.html

CONSIDER THIS! PRESENT THIS!

Make a public service announcement in which you cite your research findings about paper vs. plastic bags. Don't forget the option of reusable bags! Your announcement may be in the form of audio, podcast, radio text, graphics, tweet for print, or video for television.

GO THE **EXTRA** MILE! Find out what it would take to replace something disposable with something "green." For example, research the cost of cloth grocery bags—in terms of fabric, energy required to make them, labor, costs of transport, etc.,—and compare it with the cost of plastic grocery bags. How do you determine how good or bad something is for the environment?

BREACH OF ETIQUETTE

(Study the public's response to littering)

TIME NEEDED >
one to three days

SCIENCE >
social psychology

SCIENCE CONCEPTS >
scientific method,
gathering data,
quantifying subjective
data

ADULT INVOLVEMENT >
An adult partner should
be nearby—undercover!
—who can possibly
help by recording
interactions with a small
handheld tape recorder
or video camera.

the basics

THE IDEA underlying this experiment is that the stronger a rule is among our society, the more people will react when you break it. Some breach experiments have involved littering; others have looked at the responses of people who see someone picking up litter left behind by others.

the buzz

Keep America Beautiful is an organization that, among many things, keeps track of where most litter comes from. These are some of the top culprits:

- pedestrians or cyclists who do not use receptacles,
- motorists who do not use car ashtrays or litter bags,
- business dumpsters that are improperly covered,
- trucks with uncovered loads on local roads and highways, and
- household trash scattered before or during collection.

the lingo

breach experiment—an experiment in which you see what happens if you break a rule

you'll need

some **garbage**
an **adult** partner
a few **public areas** to conduct your experiment

what to do

1 **PLAN HOW AND WHERE** to drop your litter and what to drop. Consider walking through a crowded area of your town and purposefully doing the same thing on

the QUESTION >> How will people react if you litter?

the PLAN >> Compare the reactions of people around you as you litter in different areas.

every corner. (If you stay in one place, you may have to wait for the crowd to change before you can repeat the experiment, and that takes longer.) You may compare different scenarios, as well as different kinds of garbage and different surroundings. Here are a few sample scenarios:

- Change a baby on a bench and leave a dirty diaper on the bench when you leave.
- Toss a piece of trash toward a garbage can, miss on purpose, and walk away.
- Toss a candy wrapper on the ground.

2 **DO NOT ENGAGE** any passersby. In other words, make a point of not responding in words or actions to anything people say to you for a planned period of time, say 30 seconds or a minute.

3 **IF SOMEONE DOES** chase after you, again, plan not to say anything for 15 to 20 seconds once they reach you. Be sensible; if someone is aggressive, speak up immediately. Otherwise, after the specified amount of time, stop, thank them, explain your experiment, and pick up the trash.

After you have repeated this activity a few times, do you see a pattern?

CONSIDER THIS! PRESENT THIS!

Showing your video can provide a priceless experience for your audience.

GO THE EXTRA MILE! One way to run this experiment is to see what kind of litter gets a stronger reaction. Consider dropping different types of garbage in the same area over a couple of days (presuming that different people are there).

ANOTHER WAY to run this experiment is to see whether people in different public areas have different reactions to your littering with the same kind of litter. You can do this on one day if you have a way to get to several different public places.

4 **AS YOU LITTER,** you will have your partner surreptitiously (without being noticed) tape record and/or video and/or photograph your interactions with other people after you litter. What do you think people will do?

5 **YOUR PARTNER WILL** keep careful track of the reactions of the people around you, noting who speaks to you, who chimes in, who takes action, who picks up the trash, and anything else that happens.

6 **CAREFULLY DOCUMENT EACH** interaction, creating categories for people's words, attitudes, and actions. Try to create your structure with ratings in order to quantify your interactions. For example, the strongest reaction (5) might be picking up the trash and scolding you. A 4 might be telling you to pick up your own trash. A 3 might be just scolding you. What would a 2, 1, and 0 be?

WORKSHOP RESOURCES >>

Litter facts from No More Trash!
http://mdc.mo.gov/nomoretrash/facts/

LitterProject
http://www.litterproject.com/

Keep America Beautiful
http://www.kab.org

GREEN MAP YOUR TOWN

(Map your area's environmental sites)

the basics

KIDS ALL around the world have created different types of green maps to show the environmental sites in the cities and towns where they live.

TIME NEEDED > two weeks to a month

SCIENCE > geography, environmental science

SCIENCE CONCEPT > geographic information systems (GIS)

ADULT INVOLVEMENT > transportation and escorting may be needed

the buzz

Green Map Systems, founded in 1995, has seen the production of more than 600 hand-drawn, traced, or computer-generated maps worldwide, featuring everything from pocket gardens to toxic waste hot spots.

the lingo

green area—a place associated with trash, recycling, nature study, or other environmental concerns.

you'll need

high-tech method
Use a computer program like **ArcGIS** that lets you use geographic information to make a map to your own specifications
lower tech methods
Visit the **Green Map website** to see sample maps and to download tools and icons.
OR
Use a **computer graphics program** and **scanner** to adapt an existing map.
a **map of your town** or neighborhood
a **scanner**
a **computer**
a digital imaging program such as **Photoshop**
lowest tech method
Use an existing paper map and small stickers of different images and colors.

the QUESTION >> Where are the green areas near you?

the PLAN >> Study your local area to identify green areas and create a map to distribute in your area.

what to do

1 **SELECT THE AREA** on the map that you want to use for your Green Map.

2 **DO RESEARCH TO** find out what is in your area and locate area experts or interview people in your area to find where the green areas are. The answers will be the data on which you base your green map.

3 **CREATE A KEY** for your map. Assign icons or designate colors for different sorts of green places in your area and list them in a graphic box that will appear alongside your map. You can also get "official" Green Map icons at http://www.greenmap.org.

4 **ADD THE ICONS** or color symbols to the map for each place you researched.

5 **TREAT THIS MAP** as a preliminary draft. Take it to one of the experts you consulted in your research to show them what you are doing and get help adding information.

6 **REVIEW GREEN MAPS** made for other areas to see what you might learn more about to add to your map.

7 **ADD TO YOUR** map as needed.

8 **ANALYZE YOUR AREA** based on the picture your map provides. What environmental concerns are covered well in your area? What worries you? What would you like to see added? What would you like to know more about?

WORKSHOP RESOURCES >>

Communicate with other green map mapmakers and register your green map through the Green Map website.
www.greenmap.org

ArcGIS Explorer
http://www.esri.com/software/arcgis/explorer/index.html

How does a map of the green places in your area compare with the list of data you made? What difference does it make to create a "visual"?

CONSIDER THIS! PRESENT THIS!

Seek donations of printing services (or pay for printing) to create a green map for your area. You can print your own on a computer printer, or (in a larger size) by creating large slides in PowerPoint and taking them to a professional printer such as Fed-Ex/Kinko's or Staples.

GO THE EXTRA MILE! Consider ways to distribute your map in your area. You may be able to put it up on a local website or find funding support with which to print it for sale or giveaway.

WASTE REDUCTION
(How much trash do you produce each day?)

TIME NEEDED >
two days

SCIENCE >
environmental science

SCIENCE CONCEPTS >
trash footprint, personal consumption

ADULT INVOLVEMENT >
Get your parents on board with this so they don't unintentionally burden you with trash (including lunch trash).

the basics

ONE PERSON'S garbage amounts to 1.2 tons or 2,400 pounds (approximately) each year. That's 4.6 pounds a day, and much of the trash is not recycled.

the buzz

Nearly one-quarter of the nation's landfills have been closed, either because they're full or because the garbage was contaminating the water in the ground around and below them. Although more garbage—up to 70 percent of what's in landfills—could be recycled, an additional solution to the landfill problem is for individuals to produce less trash, leaving less of an environmental footprint.

the lingo

footprint—What you leave behind. Your environmental footprint refers to what you leave behind as you pass through your environment.

you'll need

a **camera**
a **notebook**
a **kitchen scale**
a cloth **tote bag**

OPTIONAL: *access to a computer*

what to do

1 **DAY ONE:** Each time you throw something out, weigh it, describe it, categorize it, and photograph it first. Make a note of

the QUESTION >> How will not being able to throw things away affect your day?

the PLAN >> Spend one day not throwing anything out. Evaluate the results.

the things you toss. What were they made of? Why did you have them in the first place?

2 **DAY TWO:** Today, do your best not to throw anything out. Follow the rules below throughout the day. Note that you'll need to keep your tote bag with you all day. At the end of the day, remove everything from your bag (unless there's nothing in there—congratulations!), photograph, weigh it, and describe it in your notes.

> Could you do this for a week? Try it! Could you have generated less trash? How? How will this experience change the way you buy things, eat, and live?

> What would you do if you couldn't throw any one item away? What else could you do with it? Could you find a way to dispose of it without putting it in a garbage container? Better yet, can you think of a way to avoid having it in the first place? What would it be like to have to carry this thing with you for the rest of the day?

CONSIDER THIS! PRESENT THIS!

> Use the weight of your Day One and Day Two trash to create graphs showing how much trash you would generate at this rate in a week, a month, a year, a decade, and so on.

> Create a tip sheet to give away telling your audience what successful methods you've learned to reduce trash.

> **GO THE EXTRA MILE!** Pass the tote bag to a family member or friend. How willing are other people to try this activity for themselves? Who generates the most trash?

The rules:

Your goal is to have AS LITTLE AS POSSIBLE left to throw out at the end of the day.

- You can't use the garbage cans at home or at school.
- You can't use public garbage cans.
- You can't use anybody else's garbage can.
- You can't give garbage to somebody else to throw out for you, flush trash down the toilet, or litter.
- You CAN recycle.
- You CAN compost.
- You CAN incinerate.
- You CAN donate usable items to charity.
- You CAN flush the toilet, with only FLUSHABLE items in it.
- You have to keep any trash you create within five feet of you.

WORKSHOP RESOURCE >>

Try your hand at shrinking a landfill at Learner.org's garbage site:
http://www.learner.org/interactives/garbage/landfill/

JUNK MAIL

(Study what it takes NOT to have junk mail thrown out)

the basics

SOLICITATIONS FOR charities show up in the mailbox every day: those envelopes containing return address labels with your parents' names (or yours), along with a request for a donation and a self-addressed stamped envelope.

TIME NEEDED > two or three weeks

SCIENCE > psychology, behavioral science, economics

SCIENCE CONCEPTS > assessing practical and emotional response to mail

ADULT INVOLVEMENT > Discuss your plan to solicit donations from friends and family with your parent or other responsible adult.

the buzz

The U.S. Postal Service delivers more than 100 billion pieces of bulk mail every year. Most of it winds up in landfills, so people who want to help protect the environment are trying to reduce the amount of mail they receive. See Resources for more.

the lingo

soliciting or solicitation—asking for donations

junk mail—pieces of mail sent in bulk that advertise products or services or that solicit donations

the QUESTION >> What kinds of direct mail get read and kept?

the PLAN >> Experiment with different mail methods for getting people's attention and goodwill.

NOTE: *You'll need a budget for this one. How much depends on the size of your study—that is, how many letters you send out. You may recoup the cost of your project with the donations you request, but you'll need some money to spend in the first place. If you earn back more than your costs, you might consider making a donation to a good cause.*

you'll need

a **computer, printer,** and **paper** for your letter OR
a **handwritten letter** and a **copy machine** for your letter
postage-paid envelope (available at the post office)
envelope with full-price stamp
envelope with five to ten stamps whose value adds up to full price

what to do

1 WRITE A FORM LETTER asking for a contribution to support your science project. Suggest a donation of one dollar. Send this letter to a list of people you know. (Get parental permission!) Don't write a personal note. Try to make all the letters exactly the same so that the variable is the person— and the type of envelope. Include a deadline by which you need the donation to complete your project on time.

2 PACK YOUR LETTERS into envelopes that are either pre-paid, have a full-price stamp, or have several stamps that add up to the correct postage.

3 KEEP A CAREFUL RECORD of what you send to each person and the date of sending. Add to your record:

- number of responses (letters back), and
- type of responses (donation? no donation? no response?)

4 **WHICH TYPE OF ENVELOPE** received the most responses? The most donations? The least?

WORKSHOP RESOURCES >>

Ohio Office of Compliance Assistance and Pollution Prevention Junk Mail fact sheet
http://www.epa.ohio.gov/ocapp/consumer/junkmail.aspx
National Waste Prevention Coalition:
http://your.kingcounty.gov/solidwaste/nwpc/bizjunkmail.htm

"

*Envelopes with **lots of little stamps** are meant to look like **somebody has spent a lot** of money.*

"

— Douglas Quine
mail analyst

Why would you contribute to a charity? Why wouldn't you?

CONSIDER THIS! PRESENT THIS!

Make a display of the junk mail that you used in your experiment. Take a poll on-site at your science fair station, asking viewers which mail they'd be most likely to open. Do their responses match up with your data?

GO THE EXTRA MILE! Analyze solicitation envelopes for these postage scenarios: printed notice saying that no postage is required if mailed in the U.S., printed notice saying that you can help by donating your own stamp, and a real stamp.

THE DIRTY DOZEN
(Monitor the level of pollution at a local beach)

TIME NEEDED ›
one month to one year

SCIENCE ›
environmental science, chemistry, animal behavior

SCIENCE CONCEPTS ›
polymers, ocean currents, watershed

ADULT INVOLVEMENT ›
permission to handle trash and regular rides to the beach

the basics

JUST ABOUT every beach worldwide now shows signs of people's reliance on plastics. The center of the North Pacific Gyre carries a sea of plastic garbage. Because wind and currents are weak there, the garbage gets stuck and doesn't flow on to other areas. The Sargasso Sea, another quiet-flow area in the center of the North Atlantic, has lots of trash floating around, too.

the buzz

Taylor Simpkins of Costa Mesa, California, age 13, kept track of tiny pellets of plastic called PPPs (pre-production pellets) that washed up on a nearby beach.

the lingo

pre-production plastic pellets (PPPs)—Sometimes called "nurdles," PPPs are little round balls of plastic about 3 mm in diameter that are used to make molded plastic objects. *U.S. News and World Report* says that a hundred billion PPPs are produced each year. They get into the water because of overly casual industry practices. They absorb toxic pollutants and, because they look like fish eggs, can be eaten by sea animals, fish, and birds, with harmful results. PPPs are called mermaid's tears by some beachcombers. You can guess why.

you'll need

bucket
shovel
string a little over 4 meters long
5 popsicle sticks, sticks from trees, or sturdy plastic straws
sieve or **net** with openings less than 3 mm wide
a **journal** or **computer** for recording data
zip-lock bags
permanent marker

the QUESTION >> What's washed up on your beach, and where did it come from?

the PLAN >> Collect, categorize, and source beachcombing findings.

The Center for Marine Conservation uses these categories to sort beach trash

1) cigarette butts
2) paper pieces
3) plastic pieces (including PPPs, see "the lingo")
4) styrofoam pieces
5) glass pieces
6) plastic food bags
7) plastic caps and lids
8) metal beverage cans
9) plastic straws
10) glass beverage bottles
11) plastic beverage bottles
12) styrofoam cups

what to do

1 **FIND AN AREA** of the beach that receives flow from a river.

2 **PLAN TO ASSESS** an area at this point of the beach over a time period from a month to a year. Make a point of visiting your area for samples at periods when there has been no rain and at points directly after rainstorms, so that you can see if there is a difference as water carries materials down the river to the sea.

3 **PREPARE YOUR SQUARE-METER MEASURER**
Tie sticks into your string at the beginning and then at the 1-m, 2-m, 3-m, and 4-m marks. When you find the place where you want to sample, you can use this measurer to lay out a 1-meter square. Jam the first stick into the sand; pull the string out to the second stick and jam that in; extend the string out at a 90-degree angle and jam the third stick in; do this again at the third and fourth stick to form a square. Jam the fifth stick in next to the first one.

FOR EACH SAMPLE:

4 **TAKE NOTE OF** the season and weather conditions at the time of each sample.

5 **TAKE SAMPLES OF** sand and dirt from your square. Note how far down you dig, say one or two inches, and replicate this when you take samples in the future, for consistency.

6 **COUNT AND CATEGORIZE** any large objects. Pour each sample into the sieve or net and sift out objects too big to fit through the screen. Count the PPPs in the sample, if any, and record this number. Create categories for everything you find, and count how many objects in each category you found.

7 **ANALYZE, ASK QUESTIONS,** and study a local map to figure out where the junk in your area comes from. Consider these sources and methods:

- landfill—blown away or washed away by rain
- sewer system—overflow can bring things from sewer systems (including items flushed down toilets) into the water system
- boats
- roads
- beachgoers

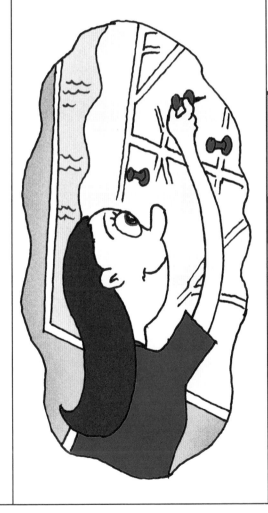

8 **STORE THE OBJECTS** you find in zip-lock bags and label them with the dates and locations.

9 **REPEAT FOR EACH** sample.

WORKSHOP RESOURCES >>

Center for Marine Conservation
www.cmc-ocean.org

"Polymers Are Forever" by Alan Weisman, Orion magazine, May/June 2007
http://www.orionmagazine.org/index.php/articles/article/270

An estimated one million sea birds and more than 100,000 sea mammals and turtles die every year because they eat or get tangled in "anthropogenic waste"—another word for litter.

CONSIDER THIS! PRESENT THIS!

Create a scientific poster of your findings. Scientific posters display the steps of your experiment. Describe your methods, and include photographs and diagrams of your process. Give your poster a title that clearly communicates your central question and your conclusion.

GO THE EXTRA MILE! Share your findings with a scientist at a local university. Go to the university website and look for a biologist, chemist, or oceanographer who might be interested in your data and have additional information to share with you.

A BLAST OF FRESH AIR
(Explore Bernoulli's principle with an old trash can)

TIME NEEDED > one day

SCIENCE > physics

SCIENCE CONCEPTS >
fluid dynamics,
Bernoulli's principle,
conservation of energy

ADULT INVOLVEMENT >
Get adult permission and
supervision if you use
the smoke bomb option.
You will also need adult
help using a craft knife.

the basics

BERNOULLI'S PRINCIPLE describes the phenomenon you can observe when you pinch a garden hose to make water squirt out: when you narrow the hose, the velocity of the water increases and the pressure decreases. The same principle applies to air that is forced unevenly through the trash can in this demonstration.

the lingo

vortex—A vortex is created when you narrow the opening of a pipe or other object through which air or a fluid (such as water) flows. This action makes the fluid at the center of the flow move faster than the fluid along the edges.

the buzz

Bernoulli's principle comes into play in many sports situations. It is the underlying principle of using uneven pressure to put a little spin or "English" on a ball—as seen in tennis, ping-pong, a "slice" or "hook" in golf, baseball's curveball, or in soccer, "bending it"—as David Beckham famously does.

you'll need

20- or 30-gallon **plastic trash can**
clear plastic shower curtain
bungee cord
scissors, craft knife
styrofoam cup
OPTIONAL: smoke bomb

the QUESTION >>

Can you use Bernoulli's principle to cause air in a tube to move at different rates and shoot a puff of air across the room?

the PLAN >>

Build an air cannon to focus air into a puff.

what to do

1 **USE THE CRAFT** knife to cut a circle 12 to 15 inches in diameter in the bottom of the trash can

2 **CUT A PIECE** of shower curtain eight inches wider than the diameter of the top of the trash can. You can do this by spreading the shower curtain on the floor, upending the trash can on it, and cutting around the edge, leaving four inches of excess material all the way around.

3 **STRETCH THE SHOWER** curtain material across the open top end of the trash can and fasten it with the bungee cord.

4 **TO WORK THE** air cannon, lift the trash can by one handle and hold it horizontally. Hold the bottom away from you. Grasp the center of the shower curtain material and pull it back, then release it quickly so it snaps.

5 **SET UP THE** styrofoam cup six inches away from your cannon. Blast it with a puff of air from your cannon. Can you knock it down? Experiment with the distance between the cannon and the cup to figure out how far away the cannon can fire the puff of air.

WORKSHOP RESOURCE >>

For an explanation and interactive animation of Bernoulli's principle, visit
http://home.earthlink.net/~mmc1919/venturi.html

> What is happening to the air inside the trash can when you snap the shower curtain membrane?

CONSIDER THIS! PRESENT THIS!

> At your science fair station, set up a target at the maximum distance at which your air cannon works. Invite visitors to operate the air cannon and knock over a styrofoam cup or other target.

> **GO THE EXTRA MILE!** You can blow smoke rings with your air cannon, using colored smoke from a smoke bomb. Do this outside! Have an adult light the smoke bomb. Set your air cannon over the smoke bomb, hole side down, until it fills with colored smoke. Lift the cannon and pull back the membrane to blow a smoke ring.

BAKING WITH SUNSHINE

(Use solar energy to cook)

the basics

YOU MAY have heard someone say the sidewalk was so hot you could fry an egg on it. Well, what can you do on a cold day? Through reflection and invention, you can actually gather and focus enough radiant energy to bake.

TIME NEEDED > one weekend to one week

SCIENCE > chemistry, physics

SCIENCE CONCEPTS > heat, insulation, radiant energy

ADULT INVOLVEMENT > get adult help or supervision when using a craft knife and spray paint

the lingo

radiant energy—energy from light

the buzz

Where have you seen this idea before? Your Girl Scout Handbook. Campers have often been called upon by their leaders to bake dessert for the troop in a solar oven. How well it works depends on how well the oven is made. See if you can beat the Scouts, then beat your own record.

the QUESTION >> How high can you get the temperature inside a solar oven?

the PLAN >> Build and improve a solar oven to find the maximum temperature you can attain.

you'll need

two cardboard boxes with flaps, one smaller than the other. The boxes should both be long and wide enough to hold a cookie sheet, and at least six inches deep.
a lid for the larger box. You can use the lid that came with the box, or you can build a lid out of extra cardboard.

craft knife
2 rolls of aluminum foil
diluted white glue (one cup of glue to one cup of water, mixed in a bowl)
paint brush
flat sheets of ¼-inch thick cardboard (you can use pieces of another box) or ¼-inch foam coreboard, cut into one-inch squares. You'll need 25 to 35 of these squares.
2 aluminum cookie sheets
2 large turkey roasting bags or 4 sheets of clear plastic about the size of the cookie sheet
duct tape
insulation material—you may use cardboard, newspaper, foam peanuts, yarn, or anything else you want to try
cookie dough (any recipe from scratch will do, or you can buy ready-made dough)

OPTIONAL: pie or cake pans to raise the cookie sheet higher, oven thermometer

what to do

1 SPRAY PAINT THE top of one of the aluminum cookie trays black. Set it aside to dry while you build the oven.

2 BUILD THE OVEN by placing one box inside the other. Use boxes that are only about one inch different in size.

A. Glue four ¼-inch-thick squares into a stack one inch thick. You may need more squares to fill the gap between your two boxes. Build six to eight stacks the right height to fit inside your biggest box so that the smaller box is held away from the bottom.

B. Using diluted glue, glue aluminum foil to the inside and outside of both your boxes, covering them neatly and completely.

C. Glue the stacks of cardboard or foam coreboard into the bottom of the larger box, evenly spaced. They will hold the smaller box off the bottom.

D. Fit the smaller box into the larger box so that about an inch is left around on all four sides.

E. Insulate the space between the two boxes, using cardboard, newspaper, styrofoam, yarn, or whatever you want to use.

F. Firmly seal the tops of the walls with duct tape.

G. Build the lid. It needs to fit securely over the top of the oven. Line it with aluminum foil.

H. Flatten your plastic bags or sheets of plastic. Measure a window one

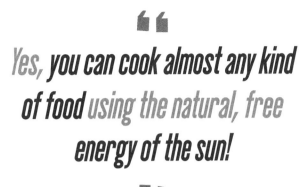

" Yes, you can cook almost any kind of food using the natural, free energy of the sun! "

— Doug Edwards
Cookwiththesun.com

inch smaller on all sides, then cut out just three sides, using a craft knife. The fourth side will make a hinge. Use duct tape to tape the plastic firmly to the inside of the lid. Note that you'll have four thicknesses of plastic, two per bag.

3 BAKE.

A. Place the black cookie sheet inside the oven on the bottom.

B. Spoon cookie dough onto the unpainted cookie sheet. Place the sheet with cookies in the oven.

C. Put the lid on the oven and adjust the window, using a ruler or stick to prop it open.

D. Set the oven in the sun.

E. **OPTIONAL:** *Insert the oven thermometer. Note the highest temperature your oven reaches and the time it takes to reach it.*

F. Adjust the window lid so that the foil reflects sun into the oven.

G. Note the time.

H. Observe your cookies through the window. Remove them when they are golden brown. Note how long this takes.

WORKSHOP RESOURCES >>

Visit the Solar Cooking Archive for many more ideas
http://www.solarcooking.org/plans/
Pizza box solar cooker: www.reachoutmichigan.org/funexperiments/agesubject/lessons/other/solar.html

Can you improve the performance of your oven by changing the insulation between the boxes, tightening the seal on the lid, or changing the time of day when you cook? What other variables might speed your baking process?

CONSIDER THIS! PRESENT THIS!

Use a time and line graph to show the increase in temperature in your oven over time.

GO THE EXTRA MILE! What else can you cook in your oven?

TRASH IN YOUR PATH

(Find patterns in street trash)

the basics

THE FACT that two conditions occur in one situation does not necessarily indicate that the conditions are related, but it is the first step to finding out whether they are related.

TIME NEEDED > several hours a week for a month for data gathering

SCIENCE > behavioral science, anthropology, archaeology, economics

SCIENCE CONCEPTS > analyzing patterns, forming hypotheses, scientific method, inquiry

ADULT INVOLVEMENT > get permission to examine or pick up trash in the street

the buzz

James Q. Wilson and George Kelling are sociologists who found a relationship between the crime rate and public disorder in neighborhoods: Clean things up and the crime rate drops; let things deteriorate and the crime rate rises.

the lingo

public disorder—To sociologists, this term may include trash, broken things, weed-filled lots, and other visible messes. Public disorder may create a sense that an area is untended and, therefore, unimportant or unnoticed. It is often related to the level of crime.

the QUESTION >> What kind of trash accumulates in your neighborhood and where did it come from?

the PLAN >> Identify an area of your neighborhood and survey and study the trash found there. Chart the different types of trash on a map, and form theories about the sources of each type of trash. Observe people's behavior in a further effort to understand trash patterns in this area.

you'll need

map of your area (you may create your own or find one online)
clipboard, paper, and pen
rubber **gloves** or surgical gloves
a **bucket**

what to do

1 **MAKE FIVE COPIES** of your area map. You will need one for each week of your study and one on which to combine all four weeks' data. (Also consider using a global information systems [GIS] map to record your data.)

2 **SCHEDULE FOUR HOUR-LONG** visits to your area.

3 **MAKE YOUR FIRST** visit. During this time walk all over the area, looking for trash that came from people.

4 **FOR THIS FIRST** visit, determine categories of trash. These categories might be based on materials (paper, metal, plastic, or fabric), or they could be based on function (food-related, lost objects, etc.).

5 **CREATE A KEY:** Assign a colored dot, letter, number, or symbol to each category and mark each place on the map where something from this category was found. You may also keep a list of things found and their locations.

6 **ADD BUILDINGS, ROADS,** and other features to your map. If you can figure out where the trash's source was, note it. (For example, if you find a lot of hot dog wrappers and there is a hot dog stand in the area, you can assume that the source of the wrappers is the hot dog stand.)

7 **ALSO TAKE NOTE** of people and vehicles and their activities in your area. Observe whether people walk through or drive through your area. Notice whether trash seems to have blown out of the back of garbage trucks, etc.

8 **DRAW CONCLUSIONS ABOUT** the activities, businesses, and habits that lead to trash in your area.

9 **FOR THE NEXT** three weeks, repeat this process.

WORKSHOP RESOURCES >>

> For more mapping, see Green Map Your Town, Workshop 6

Christopher Goodwin's blog
www. guyclinch.blogspot.com

The Garbage website
http://www.learner.org/interactives/garbage/intro.html

Analyze your map. What does it show you? How is some trash linked to roads, businesses, or other sites of human activity?

CONSIDER THIS! PRESENT THIS!

At the end of the month, create a map that includes the data from all four weeks to show changes and patterns. Consider using colored dots or other graphics to show different types of garbage.

GO THE EXTRA MILE! Deal with unusual trash in a creative way. Imagine how certain strange pieces of trash may have arrived where you found them. Return lost items if possible. Consider ways to make art from found materials!

TRASH COMPACTING

(Experiment with the volume and squishiness of trash)

TIME NEEDED > a day

SCIENCE > physics, engineering, mathematics

SCIENCE CONCEPTS > pressure, compactness, density

ADULT INVOLVEMENT > as with any appliance, have an adult handy for safety purposes and backup

the basics

TRASH COMPACTING does more than compress the amount of trash put into landfills. It also frees up garbage collectors to do other things, according to cities that use the BigBelly trash compactor in place of street corner trash cans. The BigBelly, powered by solar panels, squashes the trash so much that it only has to be picked up once every four days—instead of twice a day.

the buzz

Erik Gustafson, 11, was the youngest participant in the 2007 Discovery Channel Young Scientist Challenge. He won on the basis of his school science fair project, about water in streams, and became one of 40 students brought to Washington, D.C., to try their hands at a number of science challenges. One of those challenges was the trash compactor challenge—to compact enough bags of trash to fill a one cubic foot box. It took Erik and his team 90 minutes.

the lingo

density—a ratio representing the relationship between mass and volume. More mass in less volume equals higher density. For example, imagine a cup full of feathers. Now imagine that you compressed the feathers as much as you could and crammed more feathers into the cup until there wasn't room for any more. The volume of the cup doesn't change as you push in more feathers, but the mass of the feathers is greater, making the density in the cup higher.

Density = mass (grams) / volume (milliliters)

the QUESTION >>
How much uncompacted trash will it take to fill a box when the trash is compacted?

the PLAN >>
Measure compacted trash to figure out how much uncompacted trash you need to fill a container.

you'll need

bags of **trash**
trash compactor
table **scale**
a **cardboard box**

what to do

1 **FIGURE OUT THE** volume of the box you are trying to fill. Erik and his team used a box that was a cubic meter, but you can use this formula to calculate the volume of any box you want to use: length x width x height.

2 **WITH THE TRASH:** measure the density of each bag of garbage before and after compacting it.

To find density before compacting:

A. Determine the volume of each bag. This should be the amount it holds as given on the box, e.g. 20 gallons. Convert it to milliliters (mL), using this conversion:

1 gallon = 3.785 liters
This number is the volume.

B. Fill the bag with garbage and weigh it in grams. This number is the mass.

C. Divide the mass by the volume to get the density.

To find density after compacting:

A. Measure the compacted trash bag's length, width, and height. Multiply these three figures together to get the bag's volume.

B. You already know the mass; it won't change because you compact it, but you can weigh the compacted trash again just to confirm this fact!

C. Divide the mass by the volume to get the density.

3 **REPEAT STEP 2** with at least five bags of trash. Average the density figures for the bags to come up with an average density for a bag of trash.

4 **BASED ON YOUR** figures, estimate how many bags of trash it will take to fill the box.

5 **COMPACT ALL YOUR** trash, try to fit it into your box, and see how close your estimate was. How many compacted bags of garbage will it take to fill your box?

WORKSHOP RESOURCES >>

For more hints on trash compacting, check out "On the Implausibility of the Death Star's Trash Compactor," by Joshua Tyree, published in McSweeney's,
http://www.mcsweeneys.net/2002/01/10deathstar.html

Discovery Channel Young Scientist Challenge
www.youngscientistchallenge.com

For a description and detailed illustration of a home trash compactor, see RepairClinic.com
http://www.repairclinic.com/Trash-Compactor-Appliance-Diagram

> **"** *My mind just keeps coming up with new ideas.* **"**
>
> — Erik Gustafson

Is it a good idea to compact trash before putting it into a landfill? Why or why not?

CONSIDER THIS! PRESENT THIS!

Ask visitors to your science fair station to estimate how many garbage bags full of trash it will take to fill a given box. Keep track of people's guesses to see how good—or bad—people are at estimating trash.

Create a four-pound block of garbage with your trash compactor to demonstrate the weight of trash an average U.S. citizen generates daily.

GO THE EXTRA MILE! Experiment with different types of trash. What is the maximum amount of density you can attain by using your trash compactor to compress bags of garbage?

YES, YOU CAN!

(Experiment with soda cans to build understanding of pressure)

TIME NEEDED > a day

SCIENCE > physics

SCIENCE CONCEPTS > water displacement, water pressure, air pressure, properties of materials

ADULT INVOLVEMENT > Don't do the second experiment without an adult on hand to help and advise you.

the basics

THE FIRST soda pop cans were made from steel, but these days they are almost completely made of aluminum. They're easily recycled whether or not there's a deposit on the can because scrap metal dealers buy and sell big batches of them.

the buzz

Hydrogen Power, in Seattle, Washington, is just one company that is working on ways to convert powdered aluminum from soda cans into hydrogen cartridges that can be used as an alternate form of energy to petroleum fuels.

the lingo

demonstration—A demonstration is a replication (copy) of an experiment that asks a question beginning with "What if...?" Scientists (and science teachers and students) use demonstrations to show the outcomes of experiments and to learn about the processes on which the experiments shed light. In science, replication is the test of the truth behind any scientific experiment.

you'll need

two cans of soda—one should be a **regular** cola; the other, the **diet** version of the same cola
a **pencil**
a **saucepan**
metal **tongs**
a **stove**

what to do

Each demonstration is a test of your understanding of physics. Each one begins with a set up and a challenge question or activity. You'll need to anticipate what's going to happen, figure out how to change outcomes, and analyze what you observe.

the QUESTION >> Can you replicate these experiments involving pressure?

the PLAN >> Use two demonstrations (experiment replications) to explore the properties of soda cans and to learn about pressure.

EXPERIMENT 1

you'll need

two full, closed cans of soda—one diet, one regular
an **aquarium** or other clear storage container
water

what to do

1 **SET THE CONTAINER** on a counter so that when full of water it will be in a position where you can move around, squatting or stretching, until the surface of the water is at your eye level.

2 **FILL THE CONTAINER** with water.

3 **DROP BOTH** of the cans into the water. Observe what happens. Get your eye to the level of the water's surface. Assess and measure your observation.

CONCLUSION: What has happened? Why do you think it happened? How can you find out?

FINAL ANALYSIS: To learn about what happens in this experiment, the key concepts are density and water pressure.

EXPERIMENT 2

you'll need

a **saucepan**
water
a **stove**
a **beaker**
an **empty soda can**

what to do

Before you follow these directions, read them and answer the STOP question.

PREPARE A BEAKER of water and place it in the refrigerator to cool.

 POUR ABOUT AN inch of water into the bottom of the soda can.

3 **PLACE ABOUT A** half an inch of water in the bottom of the saucepan.

4 **PLACE THE SODA** can of water in the saucepan.

5 **HEAT THE SAUCEPAN** on the stove until the water inside the can boils.

6 **REMOVE THE BEAKER** from the refrigerator.

7 **USE THE TONGS** to remove the soda can from the saucepan.

8 **QUICKLY TURN THE** can upside down into the beaker of cold water.

STOP: What do you think will happen? Why?

WORKSHOP RESOURCES >>

For more information about aluminum soda cans, visit the Container Recycling Institute website at
http://www.container-recycling.org

For crafts you can make as you recycle your soda cans, check out the Family Crafts site:
http://familycrafts.about.com/od/aluminumcancrafts/

Side your house with soda cans like Richard Van Os Keuls. See Eco-Artware at
http://www.eco-artware.com/newsletter/newsletter_05_04.php

Get plans for turning soda cans into model vehicles at
http://www.tesscar-aluminum-craft.com/

To understand what happens in Experiment 2, the key concept is atmospheric pressure.

CONSIDER THIS! PRESENT THIS!

This workshop is a perfect one in which to display your skills with a lab report. Keep—and display—careful notes of time, temperatures, and conditions.

GO THE EXTRA MILE! Check out the can crushing device in Workshop 15, page 56.

SQUASHING ALL CARS!
(Maximize your ability to minimize a model car)

TIME NEEDED > three or four days

SCIENCE > physics, engineering

SCIENCE CONCEPTS > compression, crushing, simple machines, leverage, force

ADULT INVOLVEMENT > You need permission to destroy old cars. Ask for adult guidance with using tools, including electric drills, and with making and operating simple machines.

the basics

CARS ARE the most recycled product in America. Ninety-five percent of cars are recycled. Usable parts are removed. Metal parts are crushed, shredded, and sorted.

the buzz

In January 2007, the California Bureau of Automotive Repair began paying people $1,000 to take cars that failed their emissions tests to a car crusher, encouraging recycling at the same time as getting polluters—the state calls them "smog belchers"—off the road. The program was expected to retire 15,000 cars a year.

the lingo

cubic volume—This is an observation to make after crushing the car into a shape that is basically a rectangular prism (three-dimensional). Cubic volume = length x width x height.

PRELIMINARY EXPERIMENT

you'll need

two slices of bread
hand or electric **drill**
a nail
one steel or brass hinge
screws
scraps of plywood at least 6" x 6" square.
plywood lever—squashes car between two flat plates, with force coming through the fulcrum (hinge)

the QUESTION >>

Experiment with two or more different methods for crushing metal model cars.

the PLAN >>

Explore, discover, and experiment with different methods of compression to decide which is most effective at crushing the car, or, as they say in the recycling industry, "reducing the area of waste."

> ❝
> The car emits **high-pitched noises and then pop!** The windshield blows.
> ❞

— Ben Hewitt,
"Where Your Car Goes to Die," Popular Mechanics, *April 2007*

what to do

1 **TAKE TWO SLICES** of bread. Measure each and calculate their volume (height x length x width).

2 **USE ANY TOOLS** and materials you wish to squash one slice as flat as a pancake—or flatter, if you can.

3 **USE ANY TOOLS** and materials you wish to compress the second slice of bread into a cube.

4 **MEASURE THE PANCAKE** and the cube and calculate their volume.

BUILD BASIC CAR CRUSHER

1 **LAY THE TWO** pieces of wood flat. Use a screwdriver to attach the hinge to the edges to link them.

2 **DRILL A HOLE** of a larger diameter than the head of the nail in one sheet of plywood.

3 **DRIVE THE NAIL** into the other sheet of plywood, going through the hole. You should be able to open the top sheet of plywood freely. You'll use the nail to hold the toy car as you smash it between the sheets of plywood.

MAIN EXPERIMENT

you'll need

safety goggles

old and broken **toy cars** made of metal

two or more methods of crushing, such as

basic car crusher—follow directions in the preliminary experiment

shop vise—squashes car between two flat plates of metal with force coming from cranking a screw

platform—board that slams down onto a car from above and squeezes it between two plates

baler—machine that alternately squashes car from ends and sides to make a cube

an assortment of goods, including weights, pieces of wood, concrete blocks, bricks, rocks, and flat metal objects

NOTE: *Coming up with what to use is a major part of this experiment. As you work, you'll think of more things to try and compare.*

what to do

1 **FOLLOW THE PROCEDURE** as outlined in the preliminary experiment to squash metal cars, using the basic car crusher. Be sure to measure the toy cars before squashing, not just after.

2 **TRY ADAPTING THE** car crusher with different materials to change your outcome.

3 **TRY CREATING OTHER** basic machines or methods to change the shape of your crushed car and evaluate their effectiveness by measuring the cubic volume of the crushed car.

4 **ONCE YOU HAVE** determined which method reduces the car's volume most (pancake or cube), work on ways to reduce the volume further by compressing the car more. Experiment with materials and tools to create the most efficient car compressor you can.

WORKSHOP RESOURCES >>

For a description and discussion of car crushers, see the website How Stuff Works. Be sure to compare bale crushers, which create cubes, with crushers that merely flatten cars for transport on flatbed trucks.
http://auto.howstuffworks.com/car-crusher.htm

For an article about car crushing and a video of a car crusher at work
http://www.popularmechanics.com/automotive/new_cars/4213384.html

Compression or crushing is not the only way we recycle the steel from cars. See a car shredder in action at
http://www.youtube.com/watch?v=zHKBa_JvUAo

What works better: two moving walls (baler) or one moving wall (a ram) and one stable wall? What works better: pounding (hammer) or slowly intensifying pressure (screw vise)?

CONSIDER THIS! PRESENT THIS!

A finished bale o' car has a density of 30 to 80 pounds per cubic foot. How do you think this measurement was reached? How could you calculate it for your car compressor? Hint: Refer to the measurement of the car's volume that you made. What other measurements would you need to find the car's density before and after crushing? Check the density formula in Workshop 13.

GO THE EXTRA MILE! This experiment is based on the concepts behind a car compactor, but you don't have to use metal cars. Consider other items that must be disposed of and think of ways to compress them.

SOUNDS JUNKY

(Make trash into musical instruments)

TIME NEEDED ›
a weekend (two or
three days)

SCIENCE › physics,
engineering, ecology,
acoustics

SCIENCE CONCEPTS ›
recycling, energy
transfer, wave theory

ADULT INVOLVEMENT ›
Some assistance with
tools may be needed
depending on what
you try to make, your
materials, and the tools
you use.

the basics

JUNKYARD SYMPHONY, an "enviro-entertainment company" from Ottawa and Montreal, Canada, plays instruments made from trash and even stages a junkyard circus. "Reduce, reuse, recycle, rock!" is their motto.

the buzz

Junkyard Symphony plays mostly percussion instruments, such as buckets, cans, and a kitchen sink, but they have one string instrument—a washtub bass—and one wind instrument, a PVC pipe didgeridoo.

the lingo

percussion—two objects hit or rub together: drums, cymbals, marimba
winds—air is blown across a reed or opening: flute, clarinet
brass—air is blown into an opening: saxophone, trumpet
strings—a bow or fingers make strings vibrate: guitar, violin

you'll need

A base:
- bucket, box, furniture, broken sound equipment, pipe, mop, car parts, etc.

Additional Materials:
- shells, fishing line, used guitar strings, plastic bottles and lids, paper, wax, foil, styrofoam, etc.
- Tools to reshape with, depending on your base and materials. For instance, fashion a xylophone out of trash by varying the lengths of the strips of material you use, or drill holes in a piece of piping to make a wind instrument

what to do

1 **DECIDING WHAT TO** build will arise from what you have to build from. If you get

the QUESTION >> How can you reconfigure, reshape, or add to an object to turn it into a musical instrument, something from which a musical tone or rhythm can be drawn?

the PLAN >> Recycle something you don't need into a wind, rhythm, or stringed instrument.

stumped, take a long look at musical instruments in a shop, in your school's band room, in a book, or on the Internet. How is sound produced from these instruments? What are their materials and moving parts? What kind of energy or movement is used to play them?

2 **BUILD YOUR INSTRUMENT.** If you can, get some advice from a musician who plays the kind of instrument you're making.

3 **TRY OUT YOUR** instrument. How do you like the sound?

*The trick to finding **a good percussion instrument** is to simply go to the junkyard with a drumstick and **bang away until you find something that sounds good. Music is created by** vibration so the object must be fixed **so that it can resonate.***

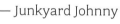

— Junkyard Johnny

Can you write a piece of music for your instrument? What part would it play in your song?

CONSIDER THIS! PRESENT THIS!

Use a computer with a program such as Garage Band that allows you to add your own musical track to an existing song. Record yourself playing your instrument.

GO THE EXTRA MILE! Start your own junkyard band.

 4 CONSIDER HOW YOU could change your instrument to change its sound. Can you tighten this, loosen that, add holes, plug holes, add or take away materials to improve its sound?

5 ANALYZE YOUR INSTRUMENT. What happens to create the sound, and how could you change it? Imagine what would happen if you introduced air, water, sand, or rice to your instrument.

WORKSHOP RESOURCES >>

Junkyard Symphony
www.junkyardsymphony.com

Garage Band software
www.apple.com

> Ideas for making trash instruments

Check out these instrument instructions and adapt them for recycled materials.
www.wannalearn.com/Crafts_and_Hobbies/Woodworking/Building_Musical_Instruments/

John Bertles
www.eco-artware.com/newsletter/newsletter_09_04.shtml

Tim Hunkins' sound experiments
http://www.hunkinsexperiments.com/themes/themes_sound.htm

Bash the Trash
www.home.earthlink.net/~jbertles/index.html

UP ON THE ROOF

(Can you insulate a house by planting grass on the roof?)

the basics

WHAT'S AN insulation workshop doing in this junkyard book? You might not think of junkyards, waste, or refuse in association with what's on the roof of a house, but think about this: The heat generated inside a house that gets to the outside is wasted, and more energy must be used to generate more heat.

TIME NEEDED >
two or three weeks
(long enough for grass
to grow)

SCIENCE > physics,
thermodynamics

SCIENCE CONCEPTS >
heat release, energy
conservation, insulation

ADULT INVOLVEMENT>
none

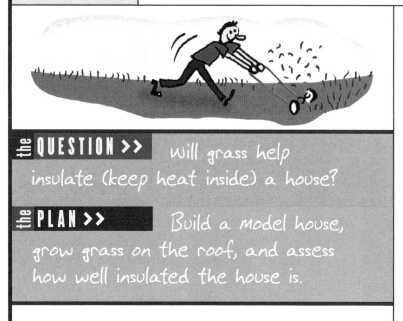

the QUESTION >> Will grass help insulate (keep heat inside) a house?

the PLAN >> Build a model house, grow grass on the roof, and assess how well insulated the house is.

> 66
> The **grass roof idea** is ancient in Scandinavia. Houses with grass roofs are **hundreds of years old**. They have huge insulating power, keep the house **cool in the summer and cozy in the winter**. Instead of putting heat into the atmosphere like a black roof, **they absorb carbons.**
> 99

— J. Alison James

describing her house and her decision to grow grass on the roof

the buzz

Chicagoans have mapped the city's "heat islands," the warmest rooftops of the city. They are warm because they have roof materials that let heat out. Chicago has plans to grow grass and trees on hundreds of these roofs. The change is expected to drop the surface temperature of roofs as much as 80 or 90 degrees.

the lingo

insulation—materials and methods for keeping the temperature stable inside a barrier—whether it's a wall keeping out the desert heat, a roof keeping the house from freezing, or a winter coat keeping the heat next to your body.

you'll need

a model house (Be creative! You can build your house of Legos, wooden blocks, scrap lumber, or styrofoam [yeah, recycle that stuff!] or use an old dollhouse, doghouse, or a wooden box.)
- Make your house a closed environment, meaning that it should be mounted on a piece of plywood, using screws, nails, glue, or tape.
- Your house should have plastic or glass to cover the windows, and

the doors should close.
- Around the roof of your house, include an edge that can hold dirt onto the roof. You can add an edge of blocks or strips of wood, and can even nail on stiff cardboard.
- You may experiment with heating the inside by putting a hot water bottle inside to raise the temperature.

piece of **plywood** big enough to form the base of your house

dirt

grass seed

a sunny indoor area

a weather **thermometer**

a sunny outdoor area

OPTIONAL: *asphalt shingles (enough to cover the top of your house)*

what to do

1 **BUILD YOUR HOUSE.** Attach it to its base, seal its windows and doors, and take its temperature. Take the temperature by placing the thermometer inside the house. Then take the temperature on the roof. Record these temperatures.

2 **CHOOSE AN AREA** in a sunny spot outside where your house can be kept for several weeks without interference from people or animals. Also choose a spot nearby that can serve as a station where your thermometer can be set up to take the temperature of the area.

3 **NOW MOVE YOUR** house to your sunny outdoor area and leave it there for two hours. During this time, leave the weather thermometer at the station. After two hours, take note of the temperature at the station before moving the thermometer to the roof of the house. Take the temperature there as well. Record these numbers carefully.

OPTIONAL: *Place a second weather thermometer inside the house to keep track of the temperature there.*

How does the layer of soil and grass change the temperature on the roof and inside the house?

CONSIDER THIS! PRESENT THIS!

Use a line graph to show the temperature at your house, at the station nearby, and inside the house. For sample line graphs, visit the National Center for Education Statistics (www.nces.ed.gov/nceskids/graphing/classic/)

GO THE EXTRA MILE! Experiment with different amounts of soil. Does adding an inch of soil make a difference to the temperature inside the house? You might plant moss or plants such as sedum on your roof instead of or as well as grass.

4 **REPEAT YOUR TEMPERATURE-TAKING** as in step 3, outside the house, inside the house, and at the station, for several days.

OPTIONAL: *Add a step by adding asphalt shingles to the roof of your house. Repeat the temperature-taking as in step 3 for several days to gather data to compare with the bare, roofed house.*

5 **NOW COVER YOUR** house's roof with one to three inches of soil. Sprinkle grass seed over the top and cover it with a thin layer of soil. Sprinkle with water until damp. You may cover the roof with plastic wrap to keep the soil damp until the grass sprouts. Then remove the plastic wrap and keep watering.

6 **ONCE YOUR GRASS** has grown, repeat the temperature-taking as in step 3.

7 **COMPARE THE DATA** that you have gathered.

WORKSHOP RESOURCES >>

Chicago Center for Green Technology
http://www.cityofchicago.org/city/en/depts/doe/provdrs/ccgt.html

The Greenroof Industry Resource Portal
http://www.greenroofs.com/

DIAPER DAN
(Test the absorbent ingredient in disposable diapers)

the basics

WHAT HAPPENS when a baby pees in a disposable diaper? The chemistry of the diaper's absorbent material changes. Different plastics are formed as different atoms are combined to make a chain of molecules called a polymer.

TIME NEEDED > a weekend (two or three days)

SCIENCE > chemistry, economics, trashology

SCIENCE CONCEPTS > polymers, absorbency

ADULT INVOLVEMENT> none

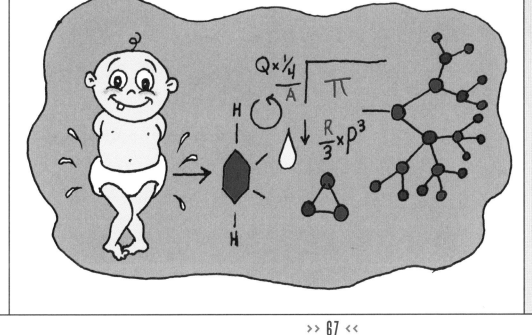

the buzz

When disposable diapers are thrown out, they're supposed to decompose. But most of them are put in landfills, where they don't get the sun and air that would help them begin to break down. It could take as long as 500 years for one diaper to decompose completely. What's more, diapers contain body waste that isn't treated as it would be if it went into the sewage system.

the lingo

polyacrylic acid—the super-absorbent polymer found in powdered form in disposable diapers. When water is added to polyacrylic acid, the acid absorbs the water and becomes a gel. Polyacrylic acid can absorb many times its weight in liquid.

you'll need

a **disposable diaper** or two
water
a kitchen **scale**
eyedropper
two beakers with volume measurements on the side

the QUESTION >>
Assess the absorbency of the important ingredient in disposable diapers.

the PLAN >>
If you have a small brother or sister or babysit for anyone in diapers, you have witnessed a diaper "burst"—that is, the fluff on the inside squishes out of the middle. Often they burst when a child wears a diaper in the pool. Through this experiment, you'll find out why this happens: experiment with the most important material in disposable diapers to learn more about how polymers work.

what to do

1 **WEIGH ONE EMPTY** beaker. Record this weight so you can subtract it later, to determine exactly how much diaper material you have.

2 **FILL THE SECOND** beaker to exactly 100 mL.

3 **DISSECT A DIAPER** to locate, remove, and identify its different parts. Look for
- the inner layer, which lets liquid through to the middle, fluffy part;
- the middle, fluffy part, which has fluff as well as a thin white powder;
- and the outer, waterproof layer.

SEPARATE THE WHITE powder in the middle, fluffy part by shaking the fluff and pulling it apart over a plastic tray. Pour the powder from one corner of the tray into a beaker.

5 **WEIGH THE BEAKER** of powder. Record this amount. Subtract the weight of the beaker so you know exactly how much powder you're using. Also note the solid measurement of the powder by looking at the scale on the side of the beaker.

 USE AN EYEDROPPER to add water drop by drop to the polymer powder. Note what happens.

7 **CONTINUE DROPPING WATER** from the water beaker into the powder beaker. Count drops carefully. If you drip a drop onto the tabletop, record that also. Later, you will check to see exactly how much water you added to the powder. Add a drop back into your water beaker if you dripped any to get the correct amount you added to the powder.

8 **OBSERVE WHAT HAPPENS** as you add water. At what point does the powder stop absorbing water? Note how many drops you have added—and determine the weight of this amount of water—before

continuing to add more water. Record your observations.

WORKSHOP RESOURCE >>

A thorough discussion of diaper construction, the history of the superabsorbent polymer in diapers, and the disposable diaper industry, is available at State University of New York at Buffalo, School of Engineering:
www.eng.buffalo.edu/Courses/ce435/diapers/diapers.html

What happens to the diaper if it is full while a baby is wearing it?

CONSIDER THIS! PRESENT THIS!

Include diapers with different amounts of water in your display.

GO THE **EXTRA** MILE! Apply water drop by drop to a new, intact diaper. At what point does the diaper "explode"? What does this tell you about what diaper manufacturers expect from diapers—and from babies? Take a look at the diaper packaging to see what the manufacturers state about their products' absorption capability.

TRASH IN SPACE
(Measure the impact)

TIME NEEDED > one day

SCIENCE > physics

SCIENCE CONCEPTS > astronaut and space program practices, projectiles, impact, kinetic energy, mass, velocity

ADULT INVOLVEMENT> none

the basics

SAY YOU have a ping-pong ball and a cannonball. Which one is going to do the most damage if it lands on the moon? You might think the answer is obvious: the cannonball. But the velocities at which things are moving in space are so high that the lightest ping-pong ball can have the impact of a cannonball.

the buzz

There are 20 tons of space trash on the surface of the moon and a lot more floating around in space. Space trash is human-made stuff left behind as a result of space exploration. Most of it is held in orbit around Earth by gravity. Sometimes it is drawn into Earth's atmosphere. Some burns up as it reenters. Other items fall to Earth. There's a danger in space trash floating in orbit because the space shuttle and satellites are up there, too, and the vehicles—or astronauts servicing them—could be hit by space trash traveling so fast that a loose paint chip could ding the window of the shuttle.

the lingo

speed—a measurement of how fast something is going on a scale of zero to whatever (it is calculated by dividing distance by time.)
velocity—a measure of the rate at which something is moving in a certain direction

you'll need

dropping area—a metal or plastic trash can, a washtub, or another container that has a bottom at least 18 inches in diameter, with sides at least 18 inches high

the QUESTION >>

How does an object's impact increase with its velocity?

the PLAN >>

Measure the differences in impact of objects of similar size but different mass, dropped from different heights (so they have different velocities), and determine how these objects might impact something they collided with in space.

dropping material—sand, flour, clay, sugar, kitty litter, or Play-Doh
balls of similar sizes—such as golf balls, ping-pong balls, etc. OR a set of balls of different mass from a science supply company (see Resources)
measuring tape with metric measurements
kitchen or lab scale with metric markings (g)
calculator

Which makes the most difference to the size of the crater: the mass the ball has or the height from which it is dropped? What about gravity? Gravity is what's keeping the objects in your experiment moving in the direction of Earth. In space, items in orbit can whiz along at 36,000 km per hour! That's quite a velocity. Although this experiment does involve gravity, the point is to look at the impact of objects moving at different velocities. You can achieve that by putting something in orbit or by dropping it with the help of gravity, as you do here.

CONSIDER THIS! PRESENT THIS!

Graph your data to show the different impacts based on height and weight.

GO THE EXTRA MILE! Use these formulas to add to your data.
Density = mass/volume
Kinetic energy = $1/2(m \times v^2)$
Velocity, $v = (2 \times g \times L)^{1/2}$
(g = acceleration due to gravity = 9.8 m/s^2 and L = drop distance)

what to do

1 **SET UP YOUR** dropping place by filling it with six inches or more of dropping material.

2 **WEIGH THE BALLS** and name or number them. If they are identical-looking, use a permanent marker to number them.

3 **BEGIN WITH THE** lightest ball. Drop it three times from each of three different heights.

4 **AFTER EACH DROP,** measure the diameter of the crater. (See illustration.) Average the three diameter measurements from each height to get the median figure.

WORKSHOP RESOURCE >>

NASA Space Trash
http://starchild.gsfc.nasa.gov/docs/StarChild/questions/question22.html

THROWAWAYS:
TAKE THEM APART!
(And put them back together)

the basics

F YOU take a close look at a piece of machinery and anticipate what happens inside it, you may be able to understand not just what it does, but how it does it.

TIME NEEDED > a day, a week, a month, or a year

SCIENCE > engineering, physics, mechanics, electromagnetics

SCIENCE CONCEPTS > machines, form and function, processes

ADULT INVOLVEMENT > You will need input from adults involving the selection of, work on, and repair of the machine you take apart. Try to find something that is still functioning but no longer needed.

the buzz

Dr. Shawn Carlson created the LabRats program, a national after-school group for exploring scientists in grades 6 through 12. This experiment is something his group does to learn and to build confidence.

the lingo

reverse engineering—figuring out how to make a machine by disassembling it. Reverse engineering is a common practice in technology because a machine's efficiency can be improved by studying its workings.

you'll need

a simple **machine**: clock, appliance, wind-up toy, etc. Yard sales are one source of discarded functioning machines.
tools

NOTE: *You'll know what you need once you start working; for example, what kind of screwdriver you might need.*

notebook and/or sketch pad or laptop computer
digital **camera**
workspace where things can be left safely (where they won't be moved)

the QUESTION >> Can you take apart a machine and put it back together so it works?

the PLAN >> Disassemble a machine, taking careful note of how the parts ~~go together~~, in what order, at what ~~tension~~ and so on, and put it back together so that it works.

NOTE: *Computer equipment, printers, and scanners should NEVER be taken apart for parts because they contain chemicals that might be harmful.*

what to do

1 **BEGIN SLOWLY TO** take apart your machine. As you work, take pictures and notes as a record of what you do.

2 **DISASSEMBLE THE MACHINE.** As you take parts off, place them in order in your work area. An important part of this process is coming up with a system of keeping track, always keeping in mind that your next job is putting the machine back together. Continue photographing and taking notes as you carefully plan what step to take next. As you do this, you're creating a "built list" that will allow you to put things back together correctly.

3 **IF YOU WANT** to test yourself, take a few parts off, then put them back. Then take them off again. This way you'll build confidence that you can put the machine back together at the end!

4 **WHEN THE MACHINE** is fully disassembled, put it back together.

5 **TEST THE FUNCTION** of the machine to make sure you have put it together properly. If it doesn't work, or works differently than before, try again.

WORKSHOP RESOURCE >>

LabRats/Society of Amateur Scientists
http://www.sas.org/labrats/index.html

Once you know your machine frontward and backward, how does this change the way you think about machines? Do you think you could fix a broken one? What do you want to take apart next?

CONSIDER THIS! PRESENT THIS!

Create a diagram of your machine to indicate what goes where and what the function of each part is.

GO THE EXTRA MILE! What if you can't reassemble the machine? Don't freak out! Take it to an engineer, an appliance repair person, an electrician, or some other genius you know. Don't let them take it off your hands and "fix it." Demonstrate your knowledge of the machine, and ask them to guide you to the point where you made the mistake and to direct you as you make the necessary changes.

PRESENT IT!

Handing It In, Showing It Off, Telling Your Story, Getting the "A"

**ERE IS** a list of things you'll definitely want to include in your table display and report for your science fair. For more, see the workshops, especially Present This! and EXTRA MILE. Here are a few general tips:

INCLUDE IT!

Your starting question(s), procedure(s), tools, data (facts), findings (results), conclusion (decision based on the facts and results), and a follow-up question should be included. Provide a list of your sources: articles, books, websites, interviews, and other information you used.

DRAW IT!

You're working with visible objects. Learn all you can by looking at them, and then communicate what you learn through your artwork. Try to show things clearly and completely.

GRAPH IT!

Computer graphics programs make it easy to put your data into graph form for easy viewing and quick communication of your findings to your audience—in some projects, this can be better than tables of data or written paragraphs. Check out these websites for making graphs:

- Statistics Canada (www.statcan. gc.ca/edu/index/-eng.htm)
- National Center for Education Statistics (www.nces.ed.gov/ nceskids/graphing/classic/)

CODE IT!

Visual representations may be more helpful than lists of numbers. As you study your area—whether it's a beach, a park, or a city block—don't just list numbers for what you find in different places. Create a graphic system in which a color or pattern stands for a certain number. You'll make your findings available at a glance.

POWERPOINT IT

Use a computer to coordinate your graphics, photographs, video, and other materials into a presentation that's quick to view and easy to understand. You can set up your PowerPoint to loop continually, present it to your teacher on a DVD, and add it to your school portfolio.
NOTE: *The Macintosh program Keynote is similar to PowerPoint.*

DRAMATIZE IT!

Consider the impact of recordings, dramatic performances, costumes, posters, sound effects, and more! There's plenty of room for creativity and drama in science.

PHOTOGRAPH IT!

Here are some tried and true tips for photographing your work:

- Still photography
- GIF file. If you have a laptop you

can bring for your presentation, use still shots to make a GIF file. Take four to six shots, then use your computer program (Adobe Photoshop, for example) to create a GIF file out of them. The program makes the stills flash by like a flipbook, so your viewer sees movement and change.

- Time lapse, when you want to capture something that takes place over time: Set up a still camera or video camera to take an image every 30 seconds. The result will be a series of still shots that seem to move and morph over time.
- Video
- Flexi-cam is a camera with a magnifying lens. It hooks up to your computer. You can aim it at anything, and it will enlarge it and put it on TV. This is a terrific way to help people see bacteria, bugs, or something else that's alive and in motion, as well as things that aren't, such as plastic pellets that have been sifted from water. Track down a flexi-cam in your school's science lab or a/v room, or see if a local university or educational cooperative has one you can borrow.

SHOW IT!
Drawings, diagrams, graphs, photographs, video, and PowerPoint presentations tell much more than you can in conversation or writing.

the resources

The International Science and Engineering Fair rules are here: http://www.societyforscience.org/Page.aspx?pid=312

All research involving humans and vertebrate animals in any facility, including schools, universities, labs, and for science fairs, requires prior approval and is subject to strict guidelines. You can find more information at these two links: http://ethics.ucsd.edu/courses/integrity/assignments/animal.html

http://www.hhs.gov/ohrp/irb/irb_guidebook.htm

WEBSITES

- Sustainable Style Foundation, about being hip and green: www.sustainablestyle.org
- American Forest and Paper Association: www.afandpa.org
- Plastics Info Center: www.plasticsinfocenter.com/?page_id=4
- Natural Resources Conservation Service: www.nrcs.usda.gov
- Kids Recycle! Tools for Zero Waste: www.kidsrecycle.org/index.php
- The Environmental Protection Agency: www.epa.gov
- The Nature Conservancy's Freshwater Initiative: www.nature.org/initiatives/freshwater
- Compost Resource Page: www.oldgrowth.org/compost
- How Landfills Work: www.howstuffworks.com/landfill.htm
- Center for Marine Conservation www.cmc-ocean.org
- Keep America Beautiful: Info on Waste Management http://www.cleansweepusa.org
- A Global Trash Menagerie: http://pem.org/sites/trash

BOOKS

The Way Things Work by David Macaulay (Houghton Mifflin 1988) and *The New Way Things Work* (Houghton Mifflin 1998)

The Down-to-Earth Guide to Global Warming by Laurie David and Cambria Gordon (Scholastic 2007)

101 Ways to Save the Earth by David Bellamy and Penny Dann (Frances Lincoln 2003)

Tracking Trash: Flotsam, Jetsam, and the Science of Ocean Motion (Scientists in the Field series) by Loree Griffin Burns (Houghton Mifflin 2007)

WHERE TO GET RID OF THINGS YOU DON'T WANT THAT OTHERS MIGHT NEED

Goodwill: anything
www.goodwill.org

The Salvation Army: anything
www.salvationarmyusa.org

AmVets: www.amvets.org

Excess Access: clothes, household items, furniture
www.excessaccess.org

New Eyes for the Needy: glasses, hearing aids, jewelry
www.neweyesfortheneedy.org

SCIENCE SUPPLIES

www.sciencestuff.com
www.sciencecompany.com
www.basicsciencesupplies.com

index